NATIONAL
GEOGRAPHIC

What Lives in a Tide Pool?

Lily Richardson

You can often find pools of water
on a rocky beach.
These pools of water are called
tide pools.
Many animals live in tide pools.
They find the food they need there.

What lives in a tide pool?

A *sea star* lives in a tide pool.
A sea star has lots of arms.
It squeezes these arms around
an animal it wants to eat.

Barnacles live in a tide pool.
Barnacles have soft bodies that are covered by hard shells.
They wave their legs out of their shells to catch food as it floats past.

A *sea anemone* lives in a tide pool.
A sea anemone has many
waving arms.
It uses these arms to sting and catch
small animals for food.

A rock crab lives in a tide pool.
A rock crab has a pair of strong
front claws.
It cracks open shellfish to eat
with these claws.

A sea urchin lives in a tide pool.
A sea urchin has a mouth with five teeth under its body.
It scrapes food off the rock with these sharp teeth.

All these animals live in a tide pool.

barnacle

sea star

rock crab

sea anemone

sea urchin

15

Index

arms	4, 8
barnacle	6, 14
claws	10
food	2, 6, 8, 12
legs	6
mouth	12
rock crab	10, 15
sea anemone	8, 15
sea star	4, 14
sea urchin	12, 15
shell	6
shellfish	10
teeth	12